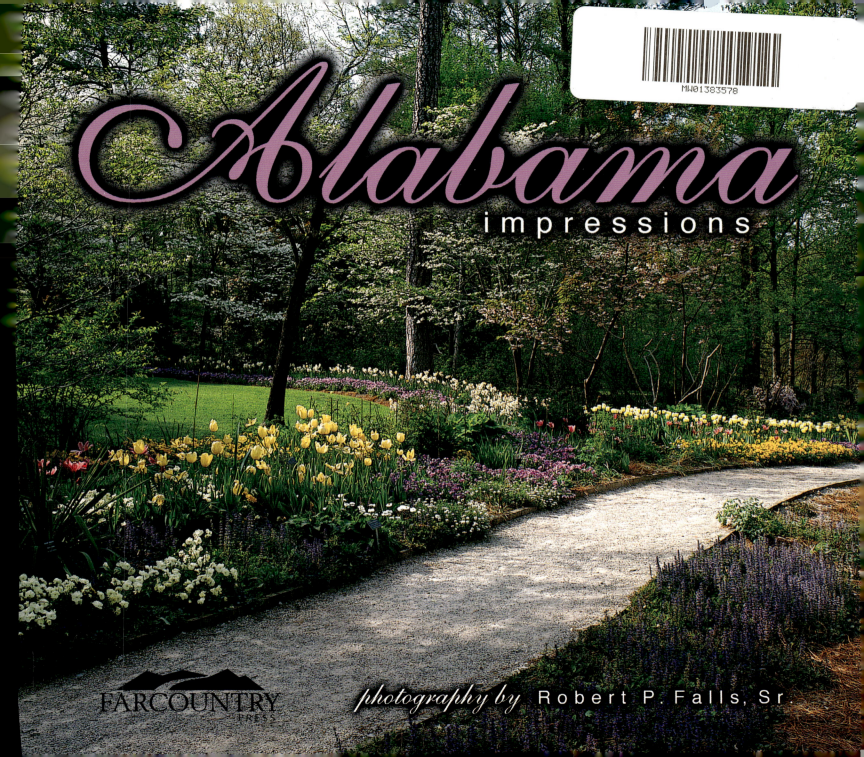

# Alabama
## impressions

photography by Robert P. Falls, Sr.

FARCOUNTRY PRESS

RIGHT: The skyline of Birmingham, largest city in Alabama, glows at twilight.

TITLE PAGE: More than 250,000 visitors per year stroll the winding paths of the Birmingham Botanical Gardens.

COVER: The Little River drops down the falls of the same name in Little River Canyon National Preserve. The river flows atop Lookout Mountain for nearly its entire length before emptying into Weiss Lake.

BACK COVER: A weathered barn and old farm implements in Etowah County hearken back to the state's early history.

ISBN 10: 1-56037-400-4
ISBN 13: 978-1-56037-400-8
Photography © 2006 Robert P. Falls, Sr.
© 2006 Farcountry Press

This book may not be reproduced in whole or in part by any means (with the exception of short quotes for the purpose of review) without the permission of the publisher.

For more information about our books, write Farcountry Press, P.O. Box 5630, Helena, MT 59604; call (800) 821-3874; or visit www.farcountrypress.com.

Created, produced, and designed in the United States.
Printed in China.

10 09 08 07 06   1 2 3 4 5

RIGHT: The original Alabama State Capitol in Montgomery was built in 1847 but was destroyed by fire in 1849. Completed in 1851, its Greek Revival replacement stands today and is world famous for its unique spiral staircase.

BELOW: A dogwood tree shows off its ivory blossoms at the Huntsville Botanical Garden, which features 112 acres of stunning year-round gardens.

ABOVE: A Civil War re-enactor bugles near Mountain Creek in central Alabama. The state seceded from the Union in 1861, becoming part of the Confederacy. It was readmitted in 1868.

LEFT: An eastern bluebird pauses on a barbed-wire fence after catching a savory treat in Wheeler National Wildlife Refuge in northern Alabama. Established in 1938, the 35,000-acre refuge is home to a variety of species, including the southernmost—and Alabama's only—concentration of wintering Canada geese.

ABOVE: Denny Chimes, on the University of Alabama campus in Tuscaloosa, rings every thirty minutes and plays songs in the afternoon. The chimes are named after former university president George H. Denny.

RIGHT: Conecuh National Forest, which occupies 83,861 acres on the border of southern Alabama and Florida, features unique pitcher-plant bogs. The carnivorous plants feed on insects they trap in their tube-shaped leaves.

ABOVE: The Arches of Friendship on Spanish Plaza were gifts from Malaga, Spain, Mobile's sister city.

LEFT: High Falls Park in Geraldine occupies thirty-eight acres and features six hiking trails and photogenic High Falls on Town Creek.

ABOVE: From high in a tree, a black bear surveys its surroundings in the Mobile-Tensaw Delta, a system of bottomland hardwoods and wetland habitats amid abundant waterways in southern Alabama. More than fifty rare and endangered plant and animal species inhabit the area.

RIGHT: A white-tailed buck grazes in 6,000-acre Lake Guntersville State Park, in the northeastern portion of the state.

FAR RIGHT: Visitors to the duck observation house at Wheeler National Wildlife Refuge can view ducks and other waterfowl in the wetlands. Located along the Tennessee River between Huntsville and Decatur, the refuge was established in 1938 to provide habitat for wintering and migrating birds.

LEFT: The Gilliland-Reese Bridge was built in 1899; in 1968, it was moved to Noccalula Falls Park in Gadsden in northern Alabama.

BELOW: A flowering crape myrtle is draped in Spanish moss near Eufaula, located in southeastern Alabama along the Georgia border.

ABOVE: Gaineswood Mansion in Demopolis was built between 1843 and 1861 by Nathan Bryan Whitfield. Designated a National Historic Landmark, the mansion is one of the finest examples of Greek Revival architecture in the United States.

RIGHT: A series of overlooks in Little River Canyon National Preserve offers visitors stunning views of the preserve, which was established in 1992 in northeastern Alabama.

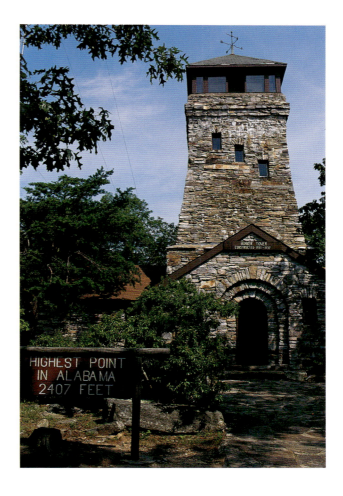

ABOVE: Bunker Tower stands in Cheaha Mountain State Park, which is the state's highest point at 2,407 feet above sea level.

LEFT: Spanning the Black Warrior River in northern Alabama, the 324-foot-long Swann Covered Bridge is the longest covered bridge in the state. It was built in approximately 1933.

ABOVE: The Barker Slave Quarters in Old Cahawba serve as a reminder of Alabama's antebellum history. Old Cahawba was the site of the state's first capital and lies near Selma in central Alabama.

RIGHT: Snow dusts the landscape surrounding Peavine Falls in Oak Mountain State Park, Alabama's largest state park at 9,940 acres.

ABOVE: This statue of Martin Luther King, Jr., stands in Birmingham's Civil Rights District. Established in 1992, the district lies at the heart of the city and includes the Birmingham Civil Rights Institute, Kelly Ingram Park, the Sixteenth Street Baptist Church, the Alabama Jazz Hall of Fame, and the Fourth Avenue Business District.

RIGHT: Opened in 1992, the Birmingham Civil Rights Institute offers exhibits on the history of racial discrimination and the civil rights movement in the United States.

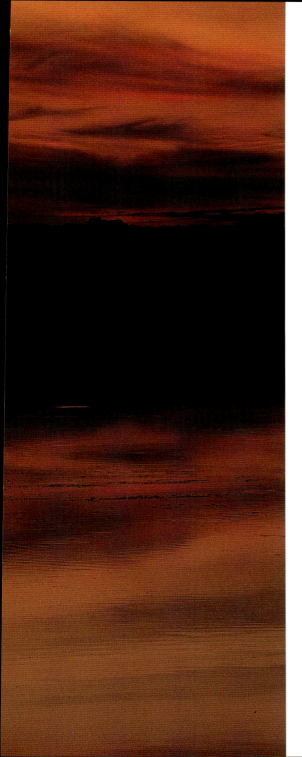
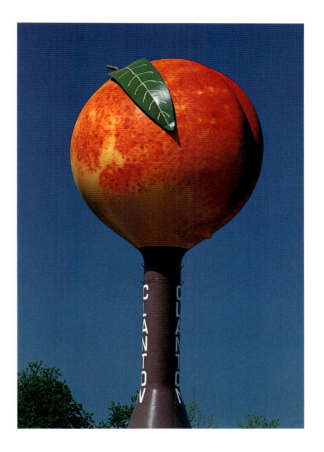

ABOVE: Clanton's peach-shaped water tower—120 feet tall, holding 500,000 gallons of water—stands as a proud monument to the state's peach-growing region in central Alabama.

LEFT: Weiss Lake reflects a brilliant sunset and a heron in silhouette.

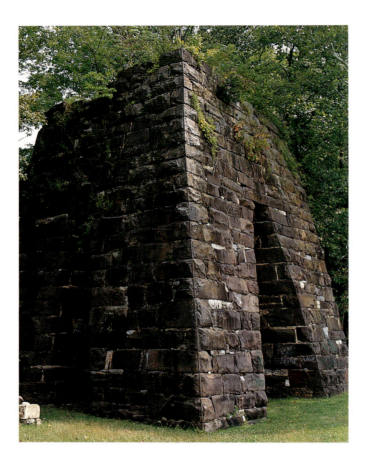

ABOVE: Built in 1862, this cold-blast furnace in Cornwall Furnace Park in northeastern Alabama supplied iron ore to foundries in Georgia, where armaments were made for the Confederacy.

RIGHT: The Southern Living Garden is one of the most striking displays at the Birmingham Botanical Gardens.

ABOVE: Located in Mobile, Fort Conde Historic Site features a replica of the eighteenth-century fort.

LEFT: A canon marks the entrance to Fort Morgan State Historic Site. The fort was used in the Civil War, the Spanish-American War, and both world wars. It played a particularly important role in the Civil War's Battle of Mobile Bay in 1864.

ABOVE: Cherokee Rock Village, also know as Sandrock, is a 200-acre park in northeastern Alabama that offers rock climbers innumerable climbing opportunities.

RIGHT: Borden Creek Trail, in the Sipsey Wilderness Area near the town of Double Springs, takes hikers to an unnamed cave behind a seasonal waterfall on Borden Creek.

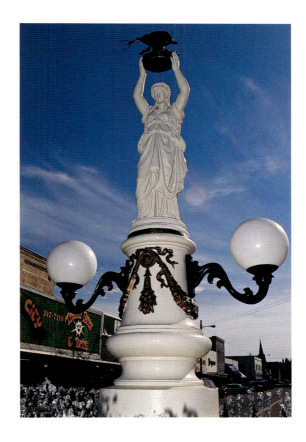

ABOVE: On December 11, 1919, the citizens of Enterprise created this unique monument to the boll weevil, a beetle that ravaged cotton fields and forced growers to end their dependence on cotton and pursue other kinds of farming.

LEFT: Wheeler National Wildlife Refuge provides winter habitat for many species of migrating waterfowl, including these snow geese.

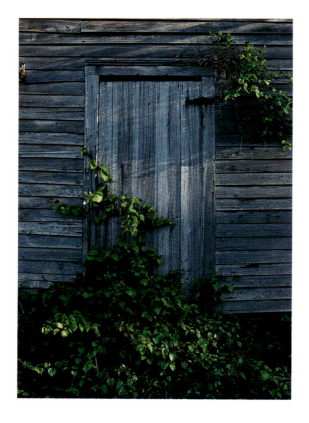

ABOVE: Vines creep around the door of a weathered barn in Salem. The town was established in 1835 and grew rapidly to become one of the state's largest cities. After a devastating fire and the Civil War, the city's government collapsed and Salem became a virtual ghost town.

RIGHT: Kudzu vines threaten to engulf this barn in Blount County. Sometimes referred to as "the vine that ate the South," kudzu vine grows at an astonishing rate in the region's climate—up to twelve inches a day!

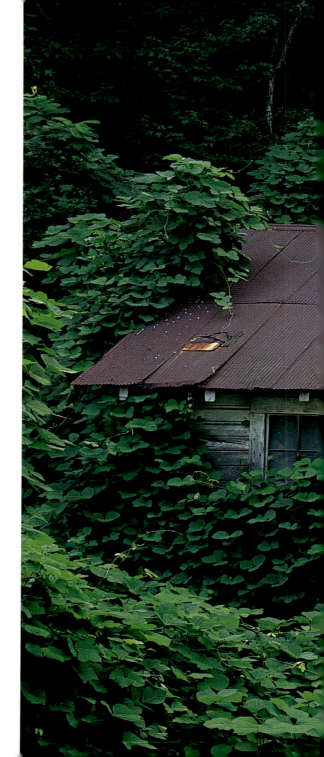

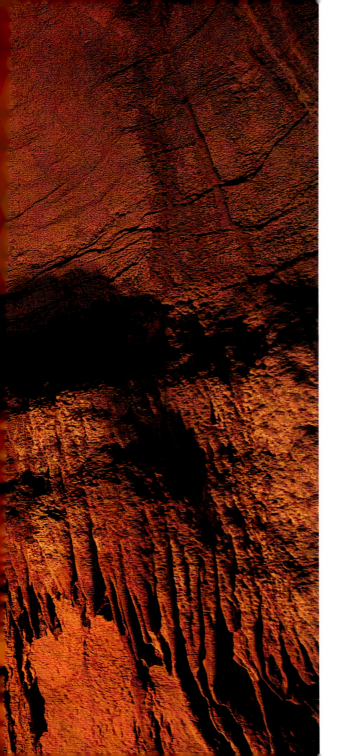

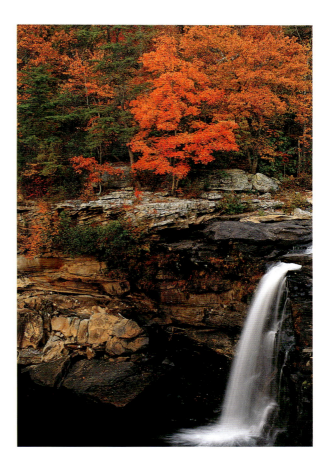

ABOVE: Fall color graces the cliffs around Little River Falls in Little River Canyon National Preserve, which occupies 14,000 acres in northeastern Alabama.

LEFT: Carved from an ancient seabed, Rickwood Caverns State Park in north-central Alabama features 260-million-year-old limestone formations, an underground pool, and blind cave fish.

ABOVE: Originally the town tavern, the Mooresville Post Office is the oldest operational post office in the state and has served the northern Alabama town since the 1840s.

RIGHT: Sunset paints the waters of the Wheeler National Wildlife Refuge in pastel colors as anglers fish for bass.

FACING PAGE: Commissioned in 1942, the USS *Alabama* now makes its home at the USS *Alabama* Battleship Memorial Park in Mobile Bay. The ship received nine battle stars for its World War II service.

BELOW: This replica of the Confederate States Navy submarine *H. L. Hunley* is displayed in Mobile. Designed and built at Mobile and named for its chief financial backer, Horace L. Hunley, it was the first submarine to sink an enemy ship; the sub was also sunk in the engagement.

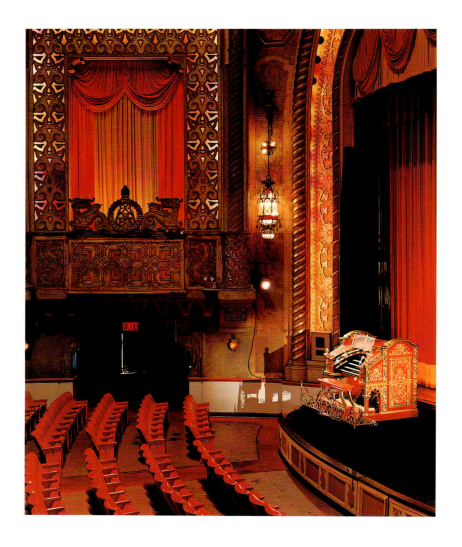

ABOVE: The Alabama Theatre in Birmingham was built in 1927 by Paramount Studios. A recent renovation has returned it to its former glory and the theater now hosts live events in addition to films.

RIGHT: Settled around 1815 and incorporated in 1890, Woodville is the oldest town in Jackson County.

LEFT: Known as the Seafood Capital of Alabama, Bayou la Batre is a leader in the commercial fishing industry.

BELOW: Sloss Furnaces National Historic Landmark in Birmingham commemorates Alabama's successful iron industry, which was sparked by James Withers Sloss when he built the furnaces in 1881 and 1882.

ABOVE: Eufaula National Wildlife Refuge was established in 1964 and occupies 11,184 acres in southeastern Alabama. The refuge provides habitat for migratory waterfowl and other birds, as well as for endangered species such as American alligators, bald eagles, and wood storks.

RIGHT: This unique rock shelter is found in the 25,986-acre Sipsey Wilderness Area, which features Alabama's only Wild and Scenic River, the Sipsey River.

LEFT: Jasmine Hill Gardens and Outdoor Museum in Montgomery features more than twenty acres of floral gardens and classical sculptures, as well as this reflecting pool.

BELOW: The camellia was named Alabama's state flower in 1959. PHOTO BY PHOTOS.COM

RIGHT: Fall color reflects in the placid waters of Lake Tranquility in Oak Mountain State Park.

BELOW: Moundville Archaeological Park is the site of a large settlement along the Black Warrior River in central Alabama that dates from A.D. 1000 to A.D. 1450.

ABOVE: A kayaker competes in a race on the Black Warrior River in northern Ala Fork joins the Locust Fork and the Sips Black Warrior River.

LEFT: Wehadkee Creek tumbles down Ro eastern Alabama near the town of Rock

ABOVE: Space Camp students at the United States Space and Rocket Center in Huntsville stay in a simulated space station called Habitat 1.

RIGHT: The United States Space and Rocket Center details space exploration of the past, present, and future. Exhibits include the *Pathfinder* orbiter, built in 1977 to test equipment and procedures for the first Space Shuttle launch. The *Pathfinder* is mounted atop the first external shuttle tank built for NASA.

ABOVE: High above Birmingham stands a fifty-six-foot sculpture of Vulcan, Roman god of fire. Giuseppe Moretti created the statue for an exhibit on Birmingham's steel industry at the 1904 St. Louis World's Fair.

LEFT: As the sun dips below the horizon, it puts on a stunning show of light and shadow at Oak Mountain State Park.

ABOVE: Beachgoers flock to Gulf Shores' thirty-two miles of sugar-white sand beaches.
PHOTO BY BUTCH DILL

RIGHT: Only footsteps remain in the Gulf Shores' beach at sunset.

LEFT: Autumn paints a stroke of bright color in this shady scene in Oak Mountain State Park.

BELOW: A log hog, this turtle refuses to share its spot along Lunker Lake with this green heron.

RIGHT: One of the most unique sites in the Five Points South district in Birmingham is the Storyteller Fountain, featuring sculpture by Frank Fleming.

BELOW: The Fort Payne Depot Museum in northeastern Alabama is housed in the original 1891 train depot. Museum exhibits feature Native American, railroad, and Civil War artifacts.

ABOVE: Tour guides dressed in period garb guide visitors through the Oakleigh Historic Complex in Mobile, an antebellum mansion built in 1833.

LEFT: The Oakleigh Historic Complex lies at the heart of the Oakleigh Garden Historic District, a group of nineteenth-century Gulf Coast and Victorian cottages in Mobile.

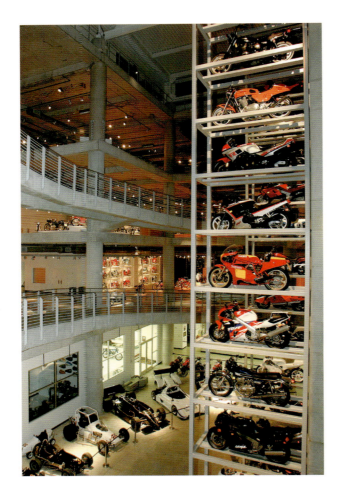

ABOVE: The Barber Vintage Motorsports Museum in Birmingham exhibits more than 900 vintage and contemporary motorcycles, as well as a large collection of racecars. PHOTO BY BUTCH DILL

RIGHT: Located north of Talladega, the Talladega Superspeedway features a track that is 2.66 miles long, the largest track in the Nextel Cup Series, and seats more than 175,000 fans. PHOTO BY BUTCH DILL

LEFT: Northeast of Talladega is Cheaha State Park, which features a lodge, restaurant, and incredible views from the highest point in Alabama.

BELOW: Cherokee Rock Village in northeastern Alabama promises sweeping views from Lookout Mountain.

RIGHT: The manicured grounds of the Birmingham Botanical Gardens welcome visitors from around the country.

BELOW: An extremely rare species in Alabama, the cahaba lily displays showy yet delicate white flowers in May and June.

ABOVE: An abandoned building recalls the past in Blount County.

LEFT: Several old barns along highways in Alabama advertise Rock City in Tennessee, including this one in Dekalb County.

RIGHT: The Big Apple or the Big Easy—signs on an old barn in Cherokee County point out the different routes.

BELOW: Jazz musician Eric Essex performs at an outdoor festival in Birmingham.

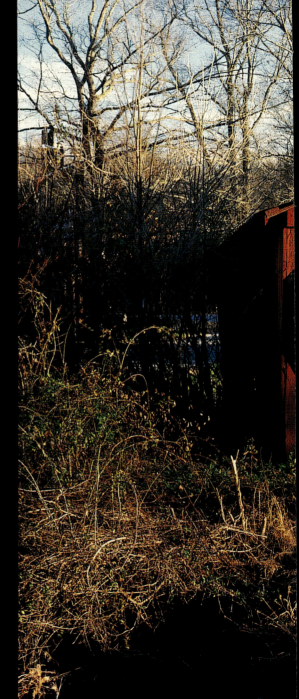

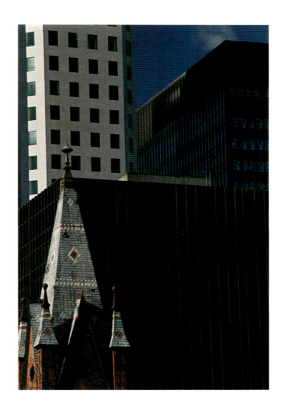

ABOVE: A study in architectural and historical contrasts in downtown Birmingham.

LEFT: The downtown Birmingham skyline appears under the arc of one of its busy overpasses.

ABOVE: Cotton was the foundation of the Alabama economy in the late nineteenth and early twentieth centuries and remains an important crop today.
PHOTO BY PHOTOS.COM

RIGHT: Opened in 1910, Birmingham's beloved Rickwood Field is one of the oldest baseball stadiums in the United States.

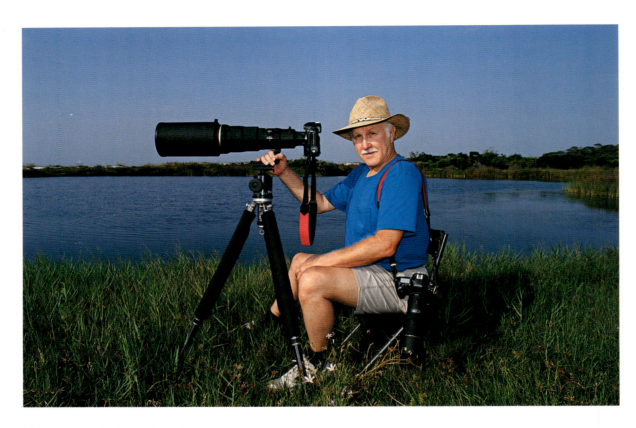

ROBERT P. FALLS, SR., is a professional wildlife, nature, and travel photographer who also writes about environmental subjects. Robert's photographs appear in books by National Geographic Books, Abbeville Publishing, National Wildlife Federation, Chanticleer Publishing, and the Audubon Society. Magazines that have featured Robert's work include *Outdoor Photographer, Nature Photographer, Outside Magazine, Outdoor Life,* and *Outdoor Traveler*. The National Park Service features Robert's images in their publications at two park locations, and the U.S. Postal Service has used one of his images on a postage stamp.